I0201895

CHAPTER ONE: THE GLORIES OF CHRIST

———

The Psalmist said, "The LORD is the portion of mine inheritance and of my cup" (Psalm 16:5) - those who know the Lord have a rich inheritance and a full and overflowing cup. It's good to meditate upon the glories of the One whom we have come to know and love and who has achieved for us such a mighty deliverance from the power of sin and Satan, and on whom the future fulfillment of those precious and exceeding great promises given to us depends. Our hearts will rejoice, our faith will be strengthened, and our love will grow warm towards our great Redeemer as we meditate on His glories and excellencies.

We are told twice in the Scriptures that God is "the God of glory" (Acts 7:2; Psalm 29:3), and we can think about both His "inherent glory" and His "manifested glory". The Psalmist said, "O LORD my God, Thou art very great; Thou art clothed with honour and majesty. Who coverest Thyself with light as with a garment" (Psalm 104:1-2); and Paul wrote of Him as "dwelling in light unapproachable; whom no man hath seen, nor can see" (1 Timothy 6:16).

"Show me, I pray Thee, Thy glory," said Moses. God answered: "Thou canst not see My face: for man shall not see Me and live. It shalt come to pass, white My glory passeth by, that I wilt put thee

1

in a cleft of the rock, and wilt cover thee with Mine hand until I have passed by: and I will take away Mine hand, and thou shalt see My back: but My face shall not be seen" (Exodus 33:18-28).

Man's vision of the glory of God, and his knowledge and understanding of the Divine Being, are very limited indeed. Humans can't for one moment sustain the ineffable, original glory of the Infinite, as the writer of this hymn says:

"Holy and Infinite, viewless, eternal,

Veiled in the glory that none can sustain,

None comprehendeth Thy Being supernal,

Nor can the heaven of heavens contain."

THE EFFULGENCE OF HIS GLORY

While it's true that man is limited in his understanding and knowledge of God, there is One who not only knows the Father fully and completely, but who is capable of bearing the absolute fullness of the glory of Deity. This One is the Son, co-equal and co-eternal with the Father Himself - uncreated and possessing the underived and unbestowed glory of Deity (Hebrews 1:1-2).

"Who being" denotes the unchanging fact of His eternal Being. He never became; He always was and always remains the effulgence of His glory. He is the revealer of God, the radiation and outshining of the character, nature and being of the Infinite.

THE GLORIES AND THE

EXCELLENCIES OF CHRIST

F. McCORMICK

Copyright © Hayes Press 2015

All rights reserved. No part of this book may be reproduced, stored in a retrieval system, or transmitted in any form, without the written permission of Hayes Press.

Published by:

HAYES PRESS Publisher, Resources & Media,

The Barn, Flaxlands

Royal Wootton Bassett

Swindon, SN4 8DY

United Kingdom

www.hayespress.org

Unless otherwise indicated, all Scripture quotations are from the Revised Version Bible (1885, Public Domain).

Table of Contents

"Being (originally) in the form of God" in the essence of His nature - for only One who is God can contain in Himself, and display, the glory of Deity in its fullness. "The effulgence of His glory, the very image of His substance" - it is evident therefore that the process of divine revelation and appearance is through the Son. Before any created being or thing external to the Godhead existed, the Triune God, (Father, Son and Holy Spirit) existed in the glory of their original Being in perfect equality, unity and bliss - one God. Even then, the Father could behold in the Son His own perfect image and the Father's glory radiated through Him - the outshining effulgence of His glory and the very image of His substance.

THE LORD AND KING OF GLORY (1 Corinthians 2:8; Psalm 24)

It is said of created things, "because of Thy will they were, and were created" (Revelation 4:11). Creation is the result of the exercise of the Divine will and the first of all created beings are the heavenly hosts, who already existed when the foundations of the earth were laid as Job 38 informs us: "When the morning stars sang together, and all the sons of God shouted for joy."

Colossians 1:16 tells us that "in Him were all things created, in the heavens and upon the earth, things visible and things invisible, whether thrones or dominions or principalities or powers; all things have been created through Him, and unto Him." John 1:3 says, "Without Him was not anything made that hath been made". His treasures of wisdom and knowledge are displayed in the works of His hands, revealing infinite knowledge and omnipotence. The marvellous designs of

Creation's works are truly past tracing out: "O LORD, how manifold are Thy works! In wisdom hast Thou made them all: The earth is full of Thy riches" (Psalm 104:24).

The believer may see something of the glories of Christ in the works of creation and admire His handiwork with adoring wonder because: "The heavens declare the glory of God; and the firmament shows His handiwork" (Psalm 19:1). David was led to exclaim, when he considered the heavens, "What is man, that Thou art mindful of Him?" The everlasting power and divinity of the Creator are clearly seen, being perceived through the things that are made, and it was the Creator incarnate who "made purification of sins" (Hebrews 1:3).

Isaiah "saw His glory; and he spake of Him," says John 12:41. He said, "I saw the Lord sitting upon a throne, high and lifted up", and "mine eyes have seen the King, the LORD of hosts" (Isaiah 6:1-5). Among the vast host of heavenly inhabitants, the seraphim are seen standing above Him with wing-covered faces and feet, as though unworthy (even in their sinless state) to look upon the majestic glory of the enthroned King, or to walk before Him with the dignity required of such transcendent greatness.

"And one cried unto another, and said, Holy, holy, holy, is the LORD of hosts: the whole earth is full of His glory." Here we see the glories of His throne linked with the glories of His Creatorship, and we know He will one day take full possession of all created things on the basis of His mighty redemptive work and the authority and power of His throne (see Hebrews 2:7-8; 1 Corinthians 15:27-28; Revelation 12:10).

He is the LORD of hosts and the Lord and King of glory, who "doeth according to His will in the army of heaven," amidst the innumerable hosts of angels. He rules and reigns amidst those sinless, holy beings in heaven as their Lord and King. He is an everlasting King, possessing Lordship over all He has made, and the inhabitants of heaven are called to "Bless the LORD, ye angels of His: Ye mighty in strength that fulfill His word, Hearkening unto the voice of His word. Bless the LORD, all ye His hosts" (Psalm 103:20-21).

Amazing grace, that He should be made a little lower than the angels because of the suffering of death yet, having triumphed gloriously over every foe, He has been "made higher than the heavens" and exalted "far above all rule, and authority, and power, and dominion, and every name that is named, not only in this world, but also in that which is to come" (Ephesians 1:21)!

He now possesses an acquired Lordship because of His redemptive work, in the sense that He has bought the field and everything in it (Matthew 13:44). "God hath made Him both Lord and Christ, this Jesus whom ye crucified" (Acts 2:36). He has Lordship over all that has been purchased at Calvary and that Lordship will one day be universally acknowledged. Even though men may now despise and reject Him, the day will come when it will be true "that in the name of Jesus every knee should bow, of things in heaven and things on earth and things under the earth, and that every tongue should confess that Jesus Christ is Lord, to the glory of God the Father" (Philippians 2:10-11).

"He is now on the right hand of God ... angels and authorities and powers being made subject unto Him" (1 Peter 3:22) ... "Who is the Head of all principality and power ..." (Colossians 2:10). The vast hosts of the angelic throng in heaven are subject to the Man of Calvary, our Lord and our Redeemer. It is written about them: "Are they not all ministering spirits, sent forth to do service for the sake of them that shall inherit salvation?" (Hebrews 1:14). We don't fully appreciate what we owe to the ministry of angels under the authority of our exalted Lord. As the hymn says:

"Swiftly they fly at His command,

To guard His own of every land,

To keep the heirs of glory."

Many scriptures speak of the ministry of angels, both to the Lord and to men, which are worthy of our meditation. Who hasn't been entranced with the scene depicted in Revelation 5? Those heavenly beings and myriads of angels say with a great voice, "Worthy art Thou ... worthy is the Lamb that hath been slain to receive the power, and riches, and wisdom, and might, and honour, and glory, and blessing ... and the four living creatures said, Amen." The hymn says:

"Amen, Amen, it rolls along,

Re-echoing from the throne again;

Be ours to mingle with the throng

In that eternal, loud Amen."

So, like a vast panorama, we can view the inherent and manifested glories of Christ from eternal ages past - "the effulgence of His glory", the glory which He had with the Father before the world was, His glory amidst angelic legions, the Lord and King of glory; then on to eternal ages future we will briefly trace "the sufferings of the Christ and the glories that should follow them".

"AND WE BEHELD HIS GLORY"

"And the Word became flesh, and dwelt among us (and we beheld His glory, glory as of the Only Begotten from the Father), full of grace and truth" (John 1:14).

Thus "we behold Him who hath been made a little lower than the angels, even Jesus" as Man a sharer in blood and flesh, the Word incarnate. We have already remarked that man could not bear the glory of God's original Being, but that glory is veiled in perfect human flesh, in Christ. It is the same glorious Person, the eternal Word through whom all things were created and are upheld, the Word which was "with God" (showing distinction) and who "was God" (showing unity) eternally. It was He who became flesh, "Immanuel," God with us, full of grace and truth.

The glory they saw was "as of the Only Begotten from the Father". God has spoken to us in His Son. His is a glory unique, unseen and unknown before among men. God the Son was before them in actual living manifestation, the Only Begotten, the perfect representation and living embodiment of the Father, revealing the attitude, character and the heart's desires of the

Father toward men, that through the Son the Father may be made known, and that men may know the Father with the object of Him being able to dwell among them (see John 17).

The Son lived amongst those who accepted Him and kept God's word, and it was they whose hearts were enlightened by divine revelation and who saw His glory. To others, there was no beauty that they should desire Him. He could say, "He that hath seen Me hath seen the Father" (John 14:9).

"No man hath seen God at any time; the Only Begotten Son, which is in the bosom of the Father, He hath declared Him" (John 1:18). Here are limitless depths and inexhaustible riches of grace and truth. "Of His fullness we all received, and grace for grace" the waves of the mighty ocean of God's blessing on the souls of men, according to the riches of His grace. Here truly is our satisfying portion for time and eternity. Oh that with enlightened eyes and hearts we may more intently gaze upon the glories and excellencies of Him who is the Image of the invisible God!

True, there were hidden beauties and excellencies which could only be seen and known by the Father in fullness, which gave God such pleasure and delight that "the heaven was opened ... and a voice came out of heaven, 'Thou art My beloved Son; in Thee I am well pleased'" (Luke 3:21-22).

"He hath declared Him" - He has told out and revealed God, who is invisible to men, not in the awful majesty of His unapproachable glory, but in human form, in love and grace. The perfect humanity of Christ is indeed proof that God had come down to speak to, and dwell among, men. No perfect human being had ever lived on earth since Adam and here was One who had a prior knowledge and existence, who knew where He came from, the purpose for which He lived and must die, and where He was going after His work here was completed. With calm majesty, He trod the pathway of suffering to the cross.

His every thought, emotion and desire were in perfect unison with the will of His Father and, in everything he did, showed to men the inward feelings, sympathy and love of God to the perishing. He lived, walked, talked and acted as God would do as a man, for indeed He was no other than God with us - "He who was manifested in the flesh" (1 Timothy 3:16). "We beheld His glory" said John, and that glory uniquely belonged to One who was the Only Begotten from the Father.

It was a glory no other could possess, and which could never be displayed by any other. He was the Prince and Head of a perfect humanity and in resurrection glory He will one day be seen as "the Firstborn among many brethren," because their Redeemer became a partaker of blood and flesh and they have become co-sharers in His triumph. (We can never of course be sharers of that unique glory which is His as the Only Begotten Son.)

He glorified His Father in life - "I glorified Thee on the earth (John 17:4), and in view of the hour of His death He asked that the Father may "glorify Thy Son, that the Son may glorify Thee" (John 17:1). Before Him lay the dread ordeal of the cross; unknown suffering, agony and shame were to be borne by Him in the loneliness and darkness of Calvary in that dreadful conflict with the powers of darkness; yet He could say, "He is near that justifieth Me" (Isaiah 50:8).

God glorified His Son in His crosswork; He showed His appreciation of that work; upholding the reputation and honour of His Son and God's favourable opinion is true glory. In that work the Son glorified the Father, vindicating God's righteousness and so laying the sure foundation by which God could come out in grace to men and fulfill His eternal counsels and purposes. In this the Father will be glorified. "The gospel of the glory of Christ" is the divine means of illuminating men's hearts, "who shined in our hearts, to give the light of the knowledge of the glory of God in the face of Jesus Christ" (2 Corinthians 4:4,6).

Well might we, who have been delivered out of the power of darkness and translated into the kingdom of the Son of His love, be found "giving thanks unto the Father, who made us meet to be partakers of the inheritance of the saints in light" (Colossians 1:12-13). It is God's purpose to conform every believer to the image of His Son in a day to come: "Whom He foreordained, them He also called … justified … and glorified" (Romans 8:30).

GOD'S PRESENT PURPOSE

While the believer is once for all secure in Christ on the ground of sovereign grace, yet God has a present purpose to fulfill here on earth in those who have been redeemed. It was this which burdened the heart of the Lord Jesus in the night of His betrayal, and in the light of His soon departure out of this world by way of the cross. He prayed:

"I pray ... for those whom Thou hast given Me; for they are Thine: And all things that are Mine are Thine, and Thine are Mine: And I am glorified in them." "Holy Father, keep them in Thy Name ... that they may be one. I pray ... that Thou shouldest keep them from the evil one. Sanctify them in the truth; Thy word is truth. Neither for these only do I pray, but for them also that believe on Me through their word; that they may all be one" (John 17).

Here is envisaged a visible unity of all disciples on earth, perfected into one or one thing by sanctification in the truth. "That the world may know ... that the world may believe that Thou didst send Me." Here is contemplated one united testimony of all believers set apart in the truth. It is sad when believers are self-pleasers and self-choosers in so-called Christendom, while these words from the heart of Christ remain on the page of Scripture.

Then He says: "And the glory which Thou hast given Me I have given unto them; that they may be one, even as We are one" (verse 22). This may be best illustrated from the shadows of the past. When God desired to dwell among His people Israel, He said, "And let them make Me a sanctuary; that I may dwell among them" (Exodus 25:8). This was to be a sanctified, or set-apart, place in which He would dwell in the middle of His people, but it had to be built according to the pattern which He Himself gave in minute detail and from which Moses was not to deviate in the smallest degree: "Thus did Moses according to all that the LORD commanded him, so did he" (see Hebrews 8:5 and Exodus 40:16).

"And the glory of the LORD filled the tabernacle" (Exodus 40:34). The glory of God rested upon the mercy-seat between the cherubim, upon the ark containing the unbroken law. God can only dwell where His will is done, and there His glory is revealed. God's glory rested in and upon His Son who was the perfect fulfiller of God's law. "Believe the works; that ye may know and understand that the Father is in Me, and I in the Father"; "It is My Father that glorifieth Me" (John 10:38; 8:54). Of whom God also said: "This is My beloved Son; in whom I am well pleased" (Matthew 3:16).

Divine approval was thus expressed, for in Him God's name was glorified, and the Son was glorified in a living witness to God's truth. He was about to leave this world and in His absence the disciples were to become God's witness-bearers as they were perfected into one in visible unity and testimony. The glory of the Divine presence was passed on to those who were found together on the day of Pentecost in obedience to His will. God's approval of them was seen in the descent of the Holy Spirit upon them, filling them all, as the glory of the LORD had filled the tabernacle. So we see a habitation of God in the Spirit, firstly in the church of God in Jerusalem, and later in the unity of all churches of God in one thing, forming one temple, one house, keeping "the unity of the Spirit in the bond of peace."

"For we are a temple of the living God; even as God said, I will dwell in them, and walk in them; and I will be their God, and they shall be My people" (2 Corinthians 6:10). This people, sanctified in the truth, are God's spiritual house in this dispensation, "the pillar and ground of the truth" in which His will is done, and godliness is the characteristic feature which should be displayed, according to the perfect pattern as seen in Him who is the Mystery of godliness. There is therefore to be the indwelling glory, and there is to be the manifested glory. In regard to the Lord Himself, there was:

(1) the divine glory (John 1:14)

(2) the glory which He had with God (John 17:5) and

(3) the glory given to Him by God, of which He said, "the glory which Thou hast given Me I have given unto them" (John 17:22).

The Psalmist could say: "LORD I love the habitation of Thy house, the place where Thy glory dwelleth" (Psalm 26:8). How true, as we think of the temple of His body, and also what should be true of all those who form part of God's holy habitation today according as it is written, "In His temple everything saith, Glory" (Psalm 29:9).

CHAPTER TWO: REFLECTED GLORY

———

"**B**ut we all, with unveiled face reflecting as a mirror the glory of the Lord, are transformed into the same image from glory to glory, even as from the Lord the Spirit" (2 Corinthians 3:18).

If we are to adorn God's temple, we must reflect the glory of the Lord. We see the glory of the Lord in the mirror of God's word, and as true reflection of His glory we are changed or transformed into the same image from glory to glory, and so we live and show Christ. This is a present, daily and progressive action. We should exercise our hearts as to whether this is true of us. Am I more Christ-like in my talk, walk, way of life and testimony than I used to be? Note how this is a vital necessity to the ministry of reconciliation - those who preach Christ must live Christ as this verse describes: "Commending ourselves to every man's conscience in the sight of God" (2 Corinthians 4:2).

The mirror of God's word gives us a perfect reflection of the glories of Christ from Genesis to Revelation, but the reflection of the excellencies of Christ by us is imperfect and partial. To produce a perfect reflected image requires a perfect reflector. It is the unevenness in the glass or metal which distorts the image; and it is the unevenness in the life and character of the child of God which distorts the image of Christ in him spiritually. The work of the Holy Spirit is to remove the roughness in the life and walk, so that more of Christ may be reflected by us. Glass or metal has to be ground and then polished to become an effective reflector; we may liken this to God's dealings with us in the grinding and polishing experiences of chastening.

What is more delightful to both God and His children than to see a truly polished Christian reflecting day by day the glory of the Lord as he is worked on by the Holy Spirit? These experiences may not be pleasing to the flesh, but they are designed for "our profit, that we may be partakers of His holiness" (Hebrews 12:10), to make us more like His own Son. This is why the writer to the Hebrews said, "My son, regard not lightly the chastening of the Lord, nor faint when thou art reproved of Him" (Hebrews 12:5).

"Consider Him", Hebrews 12:3 invites us. May it be ours to be "transformed into the same image from glory to glory"!

"Like Thee in faith, in meekness, love

In every heavenly grace

From glory unto glory changed

Till we behold Thy face."

MY GLORY

There are two great future events set out for the believer in Titus 2:13 as objectives of the Christian's hope: "Looking for the blessed hope and appearing of the glory of our great God and Saviour Jesus Christ."

The first of these will be fulfilled when the Lord Jesus comes to the air for His own according to His promise: "And if I go and prepare a place for you, I come again, and will receive you unto Myself; that where I am, there ye may be also" (John 14:8). What a blessed hope for all in Christ. He has gone, He is preparing a place and he is coming again. Shouldn't this prospect fill us with daily expectation, with yearning desire to see our Beloved? It is not merely a doctrine to be held, but a reality to be looked for. Just as much as His going to the Father was a fact, so also will be His coming for us. "For the Lord Himself shall descend from heaven with a shout" (1 Thessalonians 4:16).

In the night of His betrayal, He expressed His heart's longing in prayer to His Father, "Father, that which Thou hast given Me I will that where I am they also may be with Me, that they may behold My glory which Thou hast given Me" (John 17:24). This great event, when loved and Lover shall meet, is the subject of His promise, and prayer (John 14:17), and also of angelic and apostolic confirmation (see Acts 1:11 and 1 Thessalonians 4:15), and reaffirmed by the testimony of the risen Lord when he said: "Behold, I come quickly" (Revelation 22:12).

Are we in that happy spiritual condition which will allow us to say in truth, "Amen! Come, Lord Jesus?" Bright and glorious is the prospect before us; we, who have by faith seen that thorn-clad brow, that marred visage, and the tortured physical form of the lonely Sufferer of Calvary, "who his own Self bare our sins in His body upon the tree," shall in that moment of moments, "see Him even as He is" (1 John 3:2). Yes, we will see Him even as He is - He whom God has highly exalted, Possessor of all authority in heaven and earth, Co-partner of the

Father's throne, with glory upon glory bestowed upon Him as the victorious One in life, and in death; our Redeemer, Saviour and Lord - and His prayer and heart's desire will be fulfilled, "that they may behold My glory".

"We know that if He shall be manifested, we shall be like Him." Before we can bear the celestial splendours of our heavenly home, and gaze with wondering rapture upon that glory which God has given Him, we must know a bodily change: "For verily in this we groan, longing to be clothed upon with our habitation which is from heaven" (2 Corinthians 5:2). So "we wait for a Saviour, the Lord Jesus Christ who shall fashion anew the body of our humiliation, that it may be conformed to the body of His glory, according to the working whereby He is able even to subject all things unto Himself" (Philippians 3:20-21).

With bodies conformed to the body of His glory we shall then be able to behold His glory, which the Father has given Him. This may take place at any moment. How sad it would be if we were found, when the Lord comes, occupied with the things of this world, unfaithful, content to drift with the stream of a Christ-rejecting mass of humanity, instead of reflecting the moral image of Christ in this darkness; Then indeed we may "be ashamed before Him at His coming" (1 John 2:28).

"Are we watching for the Master?

If He should return to-day,

Would He come and find us sleeping,

As the moments pass away?"

THE APPEARING OF THE GLORY

While we are looking for the "blessed hope", we are also looking for an event which will be of world-wide importance. The "blessed hope" has to do with believers in Christ alone. It takes place in the air; it is the meeting of Christ and His Church, never more to part. This event isn't seen in Old Testament prophecy, it is a New Testament revelation. But Christ will come later, in manifest glory, to this earth to rule and reign, as is foretold from Genesis to Malachi. Of this event we read: "He cometh in His own glory and the glory of the Father, and of the holy angels" (Luke 9:26).

He is coming to establish righteous rule and government on earth, and "the government shall be upon His shoulder" (Isaiah 9:6). As for His enemies who conspire against all divine restraint, saying: "Let us break their bands asunder, and cast away their cords from us." The LORD shall have them in derision, and of Him who is seen in Revelation 19 coming forth with the armies of heaven, it is said, "Thou shalt break them with a rod of iron; thou shalt dash them in pieces like a potter's vessel" (Psalm 2).

In righteousness His kingdom will be established, and "the earth shall be full of the knowledge of the LORD, as the waters cover the sea" (Isaiah 11:9). He shall sit upon the throne of His father David: "Behold, a King shall reign in righteousness" (Isaiah 32:1). A glimpse of the glory of that future kingdom is seen on the mount of the transfiguration, of which Peter says: "For we did not follow cunningly devised fables, when we made known unto you the power and coming of our Lord Jesus Christ, but we were eyewitnesses of His majesty" (2 Peter 1:16). On that occasion God intervened from "the excellent glory" to say, "This is My beloved Son, in whom I am well pleased; hear ye Him" (Matthew 17:5). The supreme authority of Christ is one of the main characteristics of that future kingdom; His voice must be heard, and His word obeyed.

There "thine eyes shall see the King in His beauty...there the LORD will be with us in majesty ... for the LORD is our Judge, the LORD is our Lawgiver, the Lord is our King; He will save us" (Isaiah 33:17,21,32).

In that day He will be the conspicuous One among the myriads, even as He was to His own in the days of His flesh, and among the heavenly host, the altogether lovely One, appearing in glory as KING OF KINGS AND LORD OF LORDS, "and upon His head are many diadems" (Revelation 19:12). And "... He shall build the temple of the LORD; and He shall bear the glory, and shall sit and rule upon the throne; and He shall be a Priest upon His throne" (Zechariah 6:18), a Priest after the order of Melchizedek, King of righteousness, and King of peace (see Hebrews 7:2).

"Eternal glories crown His name,

As Prophet, Priest, and King;

Soon heaven and earth shall sound His fame,

Each day fresh praises bring."

But why should we be looking for that glorious appearing of which the Old Testament Scripture speaks so much? It is because that is the time "when He shall come to be glorified in His saints, and to be marvelled at in all them that believed" (2 Thessalonians 1:10), and the time also, when those precious and exceeding great promises which have been made to believers in this dispensation will find fulfillment: "If we endure, we shall also reign with Him" (2 Timothy 2:12) and "He that overcometh, and he that keepeth My works unto the end, to him will I give authority over the nations" (Revelation 2:26).

The apostle Paul, with true spiritual acumen, assessed the possibilities of having something to his account in that day of "the revealing of the sons of God," and he said: "For I reckon that the sufferings of this present time are not worthy to be compared with the glory which shall be revealed to us-ward" (Romans 8:18).

Peter said of himself in 1 Peter 5:1 that he was "a witness of the sufferings of Christ, who am also a partaker of the glory that shall be revealed". The promises made to the overcomer in the seven churches in Asia are worthy of prayerful consideration, and the words of Him whom John saw in the midst of the golden lampstands come to us with clarity and freshness: "Howbeit that which ye have, hold fast till I come ... I come quickly: hold fast that which thou hast, that no one take thy crown ..." (Revelation 2:25 and 3:11).

All believers are sharers in the "blessed hope", for the dead and living in Christ shall be changed in a moment, in the twinkling of an eye, and will be caught up to meet the Lord in the air, and so we shall ever be with the Lord. This is one of the unconditional blessings bestowed upon all who are in Christ;

but not all in Christ will be found among the overcomers. It is the present enduring sufferers with Him now, who will share those special rewards and glories with Him then.

"Now unto Him that is able to guard you from stumbling, and to set you before the presence of His glory without blemish in exceeding joy, to the only God our Saviour, through Jesus Christ our Lord, be glory, majesty, dominion and power, before all time, and now, and for evermore. Amen." (Jude vv.24-25)

CHAPTER THREE: THE HOLINESS OF CHRIST

The holiness of Christ is an eternal fact witnessed to by God, angelic beings, demons and men. Holiness is essentially inherent in His Being by reason of who he is, equally one with the Father, whom He addressed as "Holy Father" (John 17:11), and with the Holy Spirit. Of Himself it is witnessed, "Neither wilt Thou give Thy Holy One to see corruption", and again, "Ye denied the Holy and Righteous One", and again, "Thy holy Servant Jesus" (Acts 2:27, 3:14 and 4:27).

Christ is therefore inherently holy in His Deity and humanity, in Being and nature. He dwelt in the unsullied glory of eternity with the Father and the Spirit. Heavenly beings describe to each other, and in unison, as they adore and serve in the presence of the triune God, His threefold equality of holiness: "Holy, holy, holy, is the Lord God, the Almighty which was and which is and which is to come" (Revelation 4:8). Before the throne "there were seven Lamps of fire burning ... which are the seven Spirits of God". In the midst of the throne there was "a Lamb standing, as though it had been slain". Though there was divinity in manifestation, there ever remained equality of Being and attributes, and to each is ascribed that original, unimputed and eternal holiness which belongs exclusively to the triune God.

In the outworking of the divine purposes in redemption the eternal Son assumed the form of perfect humanity, which didn't affect the inherent holiness of His Person. Even though He laid aside His glory (see John 17:5), He was the same holy Being appearing in human form, revealing and displaying the moral glories which belong to Deity. He was conceived of the Holy Spirit: "Wherefore also that which is to be born shall be called holy, the Son of God" (Luke 1:35).

He was called "holy, the Son of God"; He was that before He became incarnate. The changing of His environment from heaven to earth did not alter His identity or character. The attributes of the incarnate Christ are the same as those which He possessed upon the throne when Isaiah saw Him, before whom seraphim with covered faces and feet cried, "Holy, holy, holy, is the Lord of hosts" (Isaiah 6:3). He is no less holy when veiled in perfect humanity: "Jesus Christ is the same yesterday and today, yea and forever" (Hebrews 13:8).

As Man in this world he was unique, in that He possessed a purity of nature and holiness which belonged to heaven, and this was a witness to His identity as the Son of God, and to the Father who sent Him. He lived a perfect life which could be lived by no one of the human race, for all were defiled by sin.

God gave to Israel His law which was to be lived by them as a testimony to the Name of the LORD who gave it. Alas, because of abject failure, the name of God was blasphemed among the Gentiles (Romans 2:24). The law is holy, and the commandment holy, righteous and good. It was a reflection of the divine character, but how unlike God man is. That law could only find its perfect answer in One who Himself was holy, righteous and good; that Person was Christ. He not only answered to the outward commandments of that holy moral law, but also to the inward requirements of the heart. It was his love to God and man which was the motive power of fulfillment, for He loved the Lord His God with all His heart, His soul, His strength and mind, and His neighbour as Himself. He never needed to pray like David "clear Thou me from hidden faults", for He never thought a wrong thought, never contemplated a wrong action; in Him was no sin; He knew no sin, either in mind or heart, walk or ways. No wonder He received the approval of heaven: "Behold, My Servant whom I have chosen, My Beloved in whom My soul is well pleased" (Matthew 12:18).

He was "holy, guileless, undefiled, separated from sinners". He lived in the solitude of that holy life in which none of the human race could fully share. Whilst He was loved by God and all in heaven, He was hated by men without a cause. The Holy One in their midst was a standing condemnation to the unholy and sinful, for they "loved darkness rather than light; for their works were evil." The path He trod was always in communion with the Father, and never a shadow came in between. The Father didn't limit the Spirit given to Him, and every inward movement of that Spirit found its perfect expression in the holy humanity of Christ. He lived, He walked, He worked in the power of the Holy Spirit, doing those things that he saw the Father doing (John 5:19). Finally, through the eternal Spirit, He offered Himself without blemish unto God (Hebrews 9:14).

Sinful man cannot know the abhorrent heinousness of sin because of the numbing effect of a defiled heart and mind, but He whose purity and holiness were as unsullied as when He dwelt on the throne of heaven recoiled in pain and sorrow in the presence of sin and its consequences. Isn't this the lesson written across the poignant story of Gethsemane? His utter abhorrence of sin is seen in His blood-like sweat, in the agony of soul conflict in anticipation of the cross. It is reflected in those heart-touching words of the Saviour, "My soul is exceeding sorrowful, even unto death ... O My Father, if it be possible, let this cup pass away from Me nevertheless, not as I will, but as Thou will ..." (see Matthew 26:30-45).

In anticipation, the holy, prostrate Saviour felt the pangs and pains of that dark moment in all its intensity when His holy Being would come into contact with sin as the Sin-Bearer. In that conflict of soul He triumphed and, bowing to the will of His Father, became obedient even unto death, yes, the death of the cross. The holiness of Christ was an absolute necessity to the perfection and acceptability of His sacrifice. The holiness and righteousness of God's throne were vindicated in judgement by the perfection of the holy Victim which answered every claim required by God. "Who through the eternal Spirit offered Himself without blemish unto God" (Hebrews 9:14). God's pleasure in Him is expressed in the words of the hymn-writer:

"Thou findest in that Spotless One,

Where all perfections dwell,

All that Thy heart could wish for us,

All that Thou e'er could'st tell."

God has shown His approval and acceptance of the work and sacrifice of Christ in that He has raised Him from the dead. Of that precious body in which He lived and worked, it is written: "Thou wilt not give Thy Holy One to see corruption. He whom God raised up saw no corruption" (Acts 13:35,37). "This is He which is ordained of God to be the Judge of quick and dead" (Acts 10:42). "The Judge of all is the One who in nature and character is absolutely holy, and no sin will escape His notice and judgement; the Holy One is the Son of Man" (John 5:27). "Even unclean spirits in terror-stricken apprehension asked, "Art Thou come hither to torment us before the time?" "I know Thee who Thou art, the Holy One of God" (Matthew 8:29; Mark 1:24).

To us who believe, the pattern and example of His holy life should be our objective. Let us work out our own salvation with fear and trembling, knowing that one day we shall stand at the judgement seat of Christ, before the holy, piercing gaze of the Holy One of God.

"Before the holy judgement throne

We'll see, as we in awe bow down,

Our works in fire be tried;

In view of that devouring flame,

Be this our prayer, and this our aim

In Him may we abide."

CHAPTER FOUR: THE LOVE OF CHRIST

———

The love of Christ is the most fascinating subject which has ever engaged the hearts of men, or ever reached the ears of sinful mortals. Here we find heights and depths, and lengths and breadths altogether beyond the capability of the human mind to measure. It takes us back to the dateless, timeless period of eternity past, the period when the mighty urge of divine, limitless love moved in Father, Son and Holy Spirit.

"God is love" is a statement of an eternal fact. God has a perfect knowledge of the vast cycle of eternity in which He dwells, and all the events within its vast ambit. Successive ages may run their course with all they contain; yet God has perfect knowledge of all of them. There is nothing unknown to Him that will ever take place in the flow of the years of time or the ages of eternity. It was through the Son He made or framed the ages (Hebrews 1:2). The fall of man, the result of the devil's work and man's disobedience, was within the knowledge of God before the foundation of the world. In that knowledge the love of God in Christ flowed out toward His perishing creatures, and even then redemption's plans were known. This is "the wisdom ... which God foreordained before the worlds unto our glory" (1 Corinthians 2:7). In accordance with that, God's love was to be revealed in the giving up to death of "the Son of His love," the

Lamb "who was foreknown indeed before the foundation of the world, but was manifested at the end of the times for your sake" (1 Peter 1:20).

In God's purpose He was "the Lamb that hath been slain from the foundation of the world" (Revelation 13:8) and, according to divine foreknowledge, He chose us in Him before the foundation of the world, that we should be holy and without blemish before Him in love" (Ephesians 1:4). How applicable are the words, "Yea, I have loved thee with an everlasting love" (Jeremiah 31:8)!

"From all eternity with love

Unchangeable Thou hast me viewed;

Ere knew this beating heart to move,

Thy tender mercies me pursued."

Divine love was demonstrated in two ways:

(1) by the Father giving His Only Begotten Son, and

(2) by the Son giving Himself a Ransom for all.

The Father loved the Son with measureless love, yet He "so loved the world that He gave His only begotten Son." "Herein is love, not that we loved God, but that He loved us, and sent His Son to be the propitiation for our sins" (1 John 4:10).

What it meant to God to sanctify and send His own Son into this world to suffer and die is beyond the human mind to grasp. As we meditate upon that love which gave the most loved Object of His heart, (for no one could be nearer or dearer to the heart of God than the Son, who Himself said in John 17:24, "Thou lovedst Me before the foundation of the world"), we are caused to bow in wondering worship and joy, and in holy rapture exclaim, "Thanks be to God for His unspeakable Gift" (2 Corinthians 9:15).

The Lord Jesus said, "As the Father hath loved Me, I also have loved you" (John 15:9). We may view the vast, all-inclusive orbit of divine love for the whole of the guilty race, but how sweet and precious it is to read of His personal love for the individual! How full of pathos are those words in Mark 10:21-22: "and Jesus looking upon him loved him". Love always rejoices with the truth, and when the truth was spoken in love, we read of this young man that "his countenance fell ... and he went away sorrowful." How tragic that he departed that day from One whose love would have filled and satisfied his being for all eternity, and enriched him with heavenly wealth. The present possession of earthly, vanishing riches blinded his eyes. It was not so with Paul who said, "Howbeit I obtained mercy", and "the Son of God who loved me, and gave Himself up for me ..." (Galatians 2:20). The full display of divine love is seen at the Cross.

The sacrifice of Christ was a sacrifice of love toward God and man. "Even as Christ also loved you, and gave Himself up for us, an offering and a sacrifice to God for an odour of a sweet smell" (Ephesians 5:2). He loved the Lord His God with all His heart, soul, mind and strength, and His neighbour as Himself. This love found its culminating expression at the cross, emitting a fragrant odour to God and bestowing a wealth of heavenly blessing to man. Here was love that many waters could not quench, neither could the floods drown it, a love which expended its all upon its object, loving to the uttermost, bearing all, and giving all, that object to obtain - unfathomable, incomprehensible!

"Yet there it stands. O love, surpassing thought,

So bright, so grand, so clear, so true, so glorious

Love infinite, love tender, love unsought,

Love changeless, love rejoicing, love victorious

And this great love for us in boundless store

His everlasting love - what could we more?"

That love has captivated our hearts; we have surrendered to its claims in humble contrition by accepting Christ; there is now "no condemnation"; there can be no accusation, for love has obliterated the dark record against us and is able to answer every charge, and no power in the universe is "able to separate us from the love of God, which is in Christ Jesus" (Romans 8). And now we love, because He first loved us. Love may grow, increase and abound, or it may wane and grow cold; it depends upon the spiritual condition. Paul prayed for the Ephesians:

"That ye may be strengthened with power through His Spirit in the inward man; that Christ may dwell in your hearts through faith; to the end that ye, being rooted and grounded in love, may be strong to apprehend with all the saints what is the breadth and length and height and depth, and to know the love of Christ which passeth knowledge, that ye may be filled unto all the fullness of God" (Ephesians 3:16-19).

The abiding communion of the indwelling Christ is essential to our being rooted and grounded in love, and being strengthened by the Spirit of God; our apprehension of the love of Christ may grow and expand, filling us unto all the fullness of God - glorious possibility; but perhaps so seldom realized in actual experience, because the Spirit of God within is so often grieved by unholy thoughts or words or deeds. Beloved: "grieve not the Holy Spirit of God" (Ephesians 4:30). The first fruit of the Spirit mentioned in Galatians 5:22 is love, and in 1 Corinthians 13 we find a list of things which love will and will not do, and these are worthy of earnest consideration.

It is instructive to note that Christ not only loved us as sinners, but He also loves us as disciples. Six times the term is used of a disciple, "whom Jesus loved". This too may be our happy experience, for "He that hath My commandments and keepeth them, he it is that loveth Me; and he that loveth Me shalt be loved of My Father, and I will love him, and will manifest Myself unto him." Does not this indicate a personal love to the obedient disciple - "I will love him"? Do we covet to know this intimate personal love of the Master? Paul's desire was, "That I may know Him", and here lies the secret of knowing Him. "I will love him, and will manifest Myself unto him": such is the promise of Christ (John 14:21-24). He further says: "If a man love Me, he will keep My word and My Father will love him, and We will come unto him, and make Our abode with Him."

Here is a circle of the most intimate fellowship conditioned by obedience and characterized by personal love toward each other. Oh that we may keep His word and enjoy the fellowship of such holy company! "Lord," we exclaim, "it is good for us to be here," and the Master's word to us is "Abide ye in My love" (John 15:9). May it be written across our lives and every avenue of our service - "The love of Christ constraineth us!"

We have but touched the fringe of a vast ocean. Christ loves us! "Unto Him that loveth us ... to Him be the glory and the dominion for ever and ever. Amen" (Revelation 1:5-6).

CHAPTER FIVE: THE GRACE OF CHRIST

———

The grace of Christ is inseparably linked with the display of God's attitude and purposes toward mankind. Grace was in the heart of Christ from all eternity, but was revealed in that self-humbling, self-effacing act of self-denial and sacrifice when He came in the form of a Servant in order to accomplish for man what he was unable to do for himself.

"The law was given by Moses." That law revealed the exceeding sinfulness of sin and the depths of human guilt, but "grace and truth came by Jesus Christ". "Ye know the grace of our Lord Jesus Christ, that, though He was rich, yet for your sakes He became poor, that ye through His poverty might become rich" (2 Corinthians 8:9).

It was an act of grace on His part to leave the wealth and riches of His heavenly abode and appear as a Bondservant in a spiritually bankrupt world, in order eternally to enrich men. That act originated in the gracious thought of the mind of Christ; it brought Him to the depths of poverty and destitution in order to bestow upon believing sinners, bereft of spiritual wealth, the riches of heavenly blessings. It was grace in the heart of Christ that caused Him to "leave those courts of everlasting day, and choose with us a darksome house of earthly clay." And so, "the Word became flesh ... and the Child grew ... and the grace of God was upon Him ... and Jesus advanced in wisdom and stature and in favour (grace, Revised Version margin) with God and men" (John 1 and Luke 2:40, 52).

No boy ever lived and acted as He did or dealt with others so graciously. He never succumbed to jealousy, envying or fighting, nor did He ever seek to best others to advance Himself. Ah, no. He was transparently honest, truthful, kind, considerate and gracious in all His ways and words, inside and outside the family circle. He was an example to others. He was absolutely guileless; there was nothing shady or blameworthy about Him. He was sincerely pure in thought and deed. All young disciples of the Lord Jesus should seek to be like Him.

In manhood, as Jehovah's Servant, His graciousness shines out in the beauty and sweetness of His perfect life and service. Of Him it is written "Thou art fairer than the children of men; grace is poured into Thy lips" (Psalm 45:2). He knew and saw the vile corruption of the human heart with its deception and hypocrisy, yet in compassion He spoke to men words of eternal life. He revealed God's purposes of grace toward men in preaching the gospel to the poor. His words were spirit and life. Man had never spoken like this.

At Nazareth in the synagogue He demonstrated such grace in His God-like demeanour that the eyes of all were "fastened on Him ... and they wondered at the words of grace which proceeded out of His mouth" (Luke 4:20-22). He was full of grace and truth and "he went about doing good." He had a gracious, loving approach to the needy and sorrowful. Never was there One so sympathetic and kind, so welcoming and gentle as He entered into the griefs and sorrows of others. With a tenderness of heart which was uniquely His, He displayed the grace of God as He dispensed untold physical and spiritual blessings upon sin-afflicted mortals. "Surely He hath borne our griefs, and carried our sorrows" (Isaiah 53:4).

Multitudes were enriched and blessed by His gracious ministry for "the Son of Man came not to be ministered unto, but to minister, and to give His life a ransom for many" (Matthew 20:28). Here is revealed two purposes of His coming: to minister, and to give His life as a ransom price. In life He ministered, in death He gave. Not one moment of that precious life was wasted! What a lesson! What a ministry! We gaze in admiration and wonder upon the perfect symmetry of His holy life, the perfect blending of grace and truth in all His ways. We cannot think of what He did without thinking of the beauty and glory of the Divine Worker, the Man Christ Jesus, showing omnipotent benevolence in matchless grace. He reveals Himself as the sent One of God. To us who have come to know Him He is the altogether lovely One, the Chiefest among ten thousand. He was ever the conspicuous One among the myriads of heaven, and will always remain so among the myriads of the ransomed hosts in all the perfection of His beauty and character as Redeemer, Lord and King.

The crowning act of His wondrous grace is revealed at the cross. There we behold Him as perfect Man, "crowned with glory and honour, that by the grace of God He should taste death for every man" (Hebrews 2:9). It was there the venom, hatred, malignity, and devilish cruelty, latent in the hearts of fallen men, were visible in all their fury and fullness against the gracious

Benefactor and Saviour of men. Never in this world's history were men more clearly guilty and deserving of judgement than when they became the betrayers and murderers of the Christ. Though they nailed Him to the accursed tree, they could never stop that flow of divine grace and love. From the heart of the impaled Saviour were spoken these gracious words which reached to the throne of heaven: "Father, forgive them, for they know not what they do" (Luke 23:24).

In grace He yielded His all, and the utmost depths of His poverty were reached when the Messiah, the Anointed One, was cut off and had nothing (See Daniel 9:26). God has accepted the redemption price paid by the gracious Redeemer and in answer to that plaintive cry from the cross, God, "not reckoning unto them their trespasses", offers to guilty man a perfect pardon without distinction. Peter says: "We believe that we shall be saved through the grace of the Lord Jesus, in like manner as they" (Acts 15:11).

The Lord Jesus is now the exalted and glorified One upon the throne of heaven. Because he is High Priest on behalf of His people we are exhorted thus: "Let us therefore draw near with boldness unto the throne of grace, that we may receive mercy, and may find grace to help us in time of need" (Hebrews 4:16).

Those who are saved by grace are taught by the grace of God to "live soberly and righteously and godly in this present world" (Titus 2:12). In our failure and need in the struggle, mercy and grace are ministered through One who knows by personal experience all that is involved in the path of obedience. Whatever is involved, we are encouraged to press on by His own words, "My grace is sufficient for thee." "Thou therefore, my child, be strengthened in the grace that is in Christ Jesus" (2 Timothy 2:1). "Fight the good fight of the faith, lay hold on the life eternal" (1 Timothy 6:12). "Grow in grace," and "Grace be with all them that love our Lord Jesus Christ in uncorruptness" (Ephesians 6:24).

CHAPTER SIX: CHRIST IS ALL

———

A cross the vast panorama of the fulfillment of the divine purposes relative to creation, redemption and the glories of the eternal future, we may write clearly and boldly the truth that "CHRIST IS ALL." All things find their origin and completion in and through Him: "I am the Alpha and the Omega, the first and the last, the beginning and the end" (Revelation 22:13).

Co-equal and co-eternal with the Father, He is the eternal Son: "the effulgence of His glory, and the very image of His substance (Hebrews 1:3), originally in the form of God, Himself the object of eternal love, "the Son of His love," and the object too of the adoration and worship of the innumerable heavenly hosts in the realm of eternal light. We fittingly sing:

"Of the vast universe of bliss

The Centre He and Sun;

The eternal theme of praise is this

God's Well-beloved One."

"For in Him were all things created, in the heavens and upon the earth all things have been created through Him, and unto Him; and He is before all things, and in Him all things consist (Colossians 1:16-17). He upholds all things by the word of His power. The whole universe has its existence in Him who created it, and apart from the existence of Christ in His almighty creative and sustaining power, the whole would collapse in chaotic confusion. How true that, even in creation, CHRIST IS ALL! He is the great Originator, Upholder, and Sustainer of all.

Men may try to explain the origin of the universe by the existence and operation of certain laws, but laws do not exist without a law-maker, nor can there be designs without a designer. "The world through its wisdom knew not God," but the testimony of Scripture is clear, and may be summed up in the words of John 1:3: "All things were made by Him; and without Him was not anything made that hath been made."

Of Him also it is written, "In whom are all the treasures of wisdom and knowledge hidden" (Colossians 2:8). Christ, who is the power and wisdom of God in creation, is also the power and wisdom of God in redemption. He is the Cause or "Author of eternal salvation to all that obey Him" (Hebrews 5:9). Apart from Christ, the redemption of mankind is an impossibility; our Kinsman-Redeemer must be both divine and human, able to satisfy the claims of heaven's holy throne in perfect righteousness (and only One who is divine could do that), and also to reach down to the depths of human need in liberating power and grace to release the slaves of sin and Satan.

In this matter of eternal salvation, "Christ is all" or nothing. He is the focal point of all promise and revelation. "To Him bear all the prophets witness" (Acts 10:48). "And in none other is there salvation" (Acts 4:12). If it were possible to take Christ out of the Bible as Creator and Redeemer it would become meaningless, and man would be left to grope in the darkness of night, without a glimmer of light to point him to eternal rest at last. All God's purposes of grace revolve around the glorious Person and work of Christ, and as we think of the unique position which believers occupy in the Body of Christ into which they are baptized in One Spirit, we are bound to exclaim with thankful hearts that "Christ is all, and in all" (Colossians 3:11). The slightest degree of merit cannot attach to any member of the Body of Christ for his being there; his standing there is by reason of the merit of Christ and His work of grace alone.

In contrast to the Body of Christ, which is unconditional in character, there is presented in Scripture a conditional unity of obedient disciples of the Lord Jesus, spoken of as the house of God: "But Christ as a Son, over His (God's) house; whose house are we if we hold fast our boldness and the glorying of our hope firm unto the end" (Hebrews 3:6). It is a strange thing that many, who revel in the truth of eternal salvation and of the heavenly oneness of every believer in "the Church which is His Body," fail to grasp the truth of the one thing designed by God for corporate testimony on the earth - His house.

In considering the truth of the House of God as found in Scripture we find it requires not only faith in Christ as Saviour, but obedience (1 Peter 1:2,22; 2:1-5), separation (2 Corinthians 6:14-17), conduct and behaviour (1 Timothy 3:15), and all this in subjection to "ONE LORD" (Ephesians 4:5). This is no human conception; it is found in the word of God, in "the faith which was once for all delivered unto the saints" (Jude 3). It is designed by God to be the place where His will may be done on earth, and those who find a place therein must be obedient to the words of Acts 2:41-42, which show the conditional character of a "church of God." Of the churches of God together we read, "In whom every building fitly framed together, groweth into a holy temple in the Lord" (Ephesians 2:21, RV margin).

Christ as Son is seen in supreme authority in His Lordship over the house of God. "God hath made Him both Lord and Christ" and we are to be obedient from the heart to that form (pattern) of teaching whereunto we were delivered (Romans 6:17). This is no cold formal dogma, it is a matter of the heart's attitude toward Christ in His Lordship over God's house. "Blessed is the man ... in whose heart are the high ways to Zion" (Psalm 84:5). If Christ is your all-in-all as Saviour, let us ask kindly is He your all-in-all as Lord?

Has the One who saved you been given the throne of your heart to rule and reign without a rival there? The exhortation is, "But sanctify (set apart) in your hearts Christ as Lord" (1 Peter 3:15). The supreme Lordship of Christ over God's house demands subjection and obedience, apart from which the house of God could not exist. "Christ is all" upon the cross; there can be no other Saviour; "Christ is all" upon the throne; there can be no other Lord. If we give Him His rightful place now as Lord, and go forth unto Him without the camp, bearing His reproach, He will acknowledge our obedience in a day to come. "If we endure, we shall also reign with Him" (2 Timothy 2:12).

Whatever may be understood or appreciated in the vast realms of heavenly or earthly things or beings, the truth abides that "in all things" He must "have the preeminence". "For it was the good pleasure of the Father that in Him should all the fullness dwell" (Colossians 1:19).

It is God's purpose "to sum up all things in Christ" (Ephesians 1:10). All things will ultimately find their true centre in Christ, and untold blessings will flow in "the times of the restoration of all things, whereof God spake by the mouth of His holy prophets which have been since the world began" (Acts 3:21), both in creation and toward man. His supreme Lordship and authority must then be universally acknowledged, as he is publically revealed as "King of kings and Lord of lords". All things will be subjected unto Him yet, wondrous thought, Christ, who is the sum and substance of all things in the outworking of redemption's plan, will Himself in the moment of His mighty triumph then subject himself to Him who subjected all things unto Him, "that GOD MAY BE ALL IN ALL" (1 Corinthians 15:28).

CHAPTER SEVEN: HIS RICHES IN GLORY IN CHRIST JESUS

―――

S uch are the words of Paul to the church of God in Philippi when writing that memorable letter which contains so much about the excellencies of Christ. There are references to the fact of His original Being "in the form of God", His wondrous condescension in taking "the form of a Servant", His voluntary humiliation, His perfect obedience even to the death of the cross, all emanating from His lowly, sympathetic, self-abasing mind, the mind which was in Christ Jesus in His thought for the things of others. That mighty stoop was on the one hand a display of perfect grace toward the needy and perishing, and on the other, a revelation and example of perfect obedience.

Based on this fact the exhortation is given: "Have this mind in you, which was also in Christ Jesus, not looking each of you to his own things, but each of you also to the things of others" (Philippians 2:4-5). This Christlikeness was seen in Paul, who said "If I am offered upon the sacrifice and service of your faith, I joy, and rejoice with you all." It was also seen in Timothy, of whom Paul says: "I have no man like-minded, who will care truly for your state," and in Epaphroditus also who "longed after you all, and was sick nigh unto death ... hazarding his life to supply that which was lacking in your service toward me" (Philippians 2:30).

It was the self-effacing mind of Christ which caused Him to become of no reputation, "a worm and no man", to enrich and bless others; this also characterized these faithful men. In contrast, there were those who thought only of their own things, self-centredly seeking the gratification of personal, fleshly desires; such were of those "whose god is the belly ... whose mind is on earthly things"; nothing could be more un-Christlike.

The Philippian church thought of the things of others, for they thought of the necessities of Paul in his service for the Lord. They had shown a care for him far beyond that of others and, in acknowledging the receipt of their gift, he refers to it as an ascending offering, "an odour of a sweet smell, a sacrifice acceptable, well-pleasing to God". He then adds: "And my God shall fulfill every need of yours according to His riches in glory in Christ Jesus" (Philippians 4:18-19).

The human heart and hand may fail to minister to the Lord's servants. Paul could say he had learned the secret of how "to be hungry ... and to be in want." The sweetness of this promise is to those who show that the mind of Christ is in them. "Your thought for me" resulted in "the fruit that increaseth to your account". The same principle occurs in 2 Corinthians 9:6: "He that soweth bountifully shall reap also bountifully". "And God is able to make all grace abound unto you; that ye, having always all sufficiency in everything, may abound unto every good work." "My God shall fulfill every need of yours" and whatever that need may be, there is an all-sufficiency in the risen, exalted Christ in glory to supply that need; indeed all temporal and spiritual blessings flow down to us through Him, the almighty and beneficent Lord of all.

God's riches in glory in Christ Jesus are bestowed upon those who with Christ-like mind, and purity and loyalty of heart, honour the Lord with their substance or service. They truly will know the reaping of blessings and the increase of the fruits of righteousness, and there will also be a future recompense of reward. God's people have a High Priest who is declared to be a Priest after the order of Melchizedek. He is a Priest in resurrection glory.

Melchizedek was priest of God Most High, Possessor of heaven and earth, and so is Christ. There is unlimited wealth and power at His disposal, and there can be no need beyond His competency to supply according to those riches in glory in Christ Jesus. Are we living in the present enjoyment of this exceeding great and precious promise? If we do not know this blessing, it is because we have not the mind of Christ in us actively sacrificing present gain or pleasure for the blessing of others and the glory of God. Perhaps we hold on too much to our own things for personal interests and advancement. It was not so with Christ; "He emptied Himself." He became poor that we through His poverty might become rich. He yielded His all, and countless myriads of the redeemed have through Him been eternally enriched.

He will never forget the kindness shown to those who belong to Him. It may be a prophet's reward, or a righteous man's reward: "and whosoever shall give to drink unto one of these little ones a cup of cold water only, in the name of a disciple, verily I say unto you, he shall in no wise lose his reward" (Matthew 10:41-42). In grasping present opportunities to minister to His despised and rejected people, it will result in knowing something experientially of those rich supplies which are found in "His riches in glory in Christ Jesus." "Give, and it shall be given unto you; good measure, pressed down, shaken together, running over" (Luke 6:88). Did not David remember the kindness shown to him and those with him when the people were hungry, and weary and thirsty in the wilderness during the rebellion of Absalom?

Barzillai with others provided the king and the people with sustenance in a dark day (2 Samuel 17:27-29). David never forgot this kindness to the day of his death when he then charged Solomon saying: "But shew kindness unto the sons of Barzillai the Gileadite, and let them be of those that eat at thy table; for so they came to me when I fled from Absalom thy brother" (1 Kings 2:7).

Of Solomon's servants who provided for his table it is written, "they let nothing be lacking" and when the Queen of Sheba came to Solomon and saw the meat of his table, the sitting of his servants, the attendance of his ministers, and their apparel ... there was no more spirit in her. "I believed not ... until ... mine eyes had seen it," she said, "and, behold, the half was not told me". The glory and wealth of Solomon, and the meat of his table of which the sons of Barzillai partook in the presence of the exalted king, are not to be compared with God's riches in glory in Christ Jesus, which will be displayed to myriads of wondering angels and men, which are quite beyond the human mind to grasp or describe.

The half has not been told, yet there is the present possibility of being a partaker now of these abundant supplies and also of obtaining a place near the King in that day of His manifested glory, if we are among those who have the same mind which was in Christ Jesus. "But to this man will I look, even to him that is poor and of a contrite spirit and that trembleth at My word" (Isaiah 66:2).

CHAPTER EIGHT: THE OIL OF GLADNESS

F rom whatever angle and in whatever circumstances we may view our great Redeemer, we may see fresh beauties and radiations of His glory. There is nothing that He has done, or will yet do, that will not display something of the Divine glory which uniquely belongs to Him, and in which also are manifestations of the Godhead. We have briefly made reference to God's riches in glory in Christ Jesus and it is a soul-satisfying thought that God has found in Him what satisfies the deep longings of His own heart for all eternity. There is no requirement of God's holy throne that has not found its perfect answer in the perfect life and cross-work of our Lord Jesus Christ, and there is no longing in God's heart of infinite love that has not found its full response and satisfaction in the Person of Christ. With joy we may exult and say: "Behold, O God our Shield, and look upon the face of Thine Anointed" (Psalm 84:9).

"To Him be the glory both now and forever. Amen." Indeed if this were not so, there could be no outpouring of blessing upon men. It was only when God had received His portion from the sacrifices on Israel's altars that they could receive the blessings and benefits flowing from them. God has found eternal delight in the accomplished work of Calvary and the glorious triumph of resurrection. He can look with joy upon the Man of His right hand, upon the Son of Man whom He made strong for Himself. From the terrors, horrors and darkness of the cross and tomb,

God has raised Him up and seated Him at His own right hand. Of Him it is prophetically written: "Thou shalt make Me full of gladness with Thy countenance" (Acts 2:28). He had known the bitter loneliness of being forsaken by God, the hiding of God's face, the unanswered cry in the experience of His deepest distress when it was fulfilled, "Thou shalt make His soul an offering for sin" (Isaiah 53:10).

"The head once full of bruises,

So full of pain and scorn,

Midst other sore abuses

Mocked with a crown of thorn.

That head is now surrounded

With brightest majesty,

In death once bowed and wounded,

Accursed on the tree."

Yes, the crucified One is now the enthroned One and the everlasting doors have been opened for the return of the triumphant Saviour. He has been "received up in glory," and of the Son God says, "Thy throne, O God, is for ever and ever; And the sceptre of uprightness is the sceptre of Thy kingdom. Thou hast loved righteousness, and hated iniquity; Therefore God, Thy God, hath anointed Thee with the oil of gladness above Thy fellows" (Hebrews 1:9-10). Two things are said about making Christ glad. He was made glad with the Father's countenance and He was anointed with the oil of gladness by the Father.

It makes our hearts rejoice to think that the lonely Sufferer of Calvary has been made glad with the countenance of His Father who has looked upon the battle-scarred returning Conqueror with infinite delight and approval. What joy filled the heart of the Father! What a wealth of meaning is conveyed by the countenance! It speaks volumes without words. For the Son to look upon the countenance of His Father which conveyed such unspeakable pleasure, filled Him with the fulness of gladness. As Psalm 16:11 says: "In Thy presence is fullness of joy; in Thy right hand there are pleasures for evermore." Thus we see the blessed or happy God rejoicing over the Son of His love in the knowledge that all had been completed; the basis had been laid whereby all God's future purposes of grace could righteously be accomplished. He had truly loved righteousness, even though it had involved Him in untold suffering and reproach. Nothing could or did cause Him to deviate from the paths of righteousness in the slightest degree and in this He had found delight.

"I delight to do Thy will, O My God" was the language of His heart. He was that blessed or happy Man of Psalm 1 who delighted in the law of the LORD; and in His law did He meditate day and night. There was no happier Man on earth than Him. He possessed an inward joy and a calm, unruffled peace within which no-one else knew. He was the perfect hearer and fulfiller of God's law and will. He could say, "I have glorified Thee on the earth, having accomplished the work which Thou hast given Me to do" (John 17:4).

In association with His throne and sceptre, He was anointed with the oil of gladness above His fellows. It is said in Proverbs 27:9 that "Ointment and perfume rejoice the heart". After referring to this wondrous occasion, the Psalmist then says, "all Thy garments smell of myrrh, and aloes, and cassia; out of ivory palaces stringed instruments have made Thee glad" (Psalm 45:8). And who more worthy than He to be made glad?

"And I heard a voice of many angels round about the throne and the living creatures and the elders; and the number of them was ten thousand times ten thousand, and thousands of thousands; saying with a great voice, Worthy is the Lamb that hath been slain to receive the power, and riches, and wisdom, and might, and honour, and glory, and blessing" (Revelation 5:12).

All heaven acclaims His worthiness; and of all in that holy, happy land, there is now none so radiant with joy as He, and all heaven rejoices in the honour bestowed upon their King and Redeemer. Never again will He be called upon to go out alone into the darkness and storms of a cruel, God-hating world to suffer. With joy we can now sing:

"Tis past, the dark and dreary night,

O God, we see Him now,

Our morning Star, without a cloud

Of sadness on His brow."

Why should His people then be sad? Shouldn't we catch the spirit of that anointing scene in heaven and rejoice greatly with joy unspeakable and full of glory? Should we not be showing on earth something of the joy of Christ's triumphant gladness? Our Saviour is a rejoicing Christ upon the throne, and we through Him have received "the oil of joy for mourning, the garment of praise for the spirit of heaviness." We can draw water out of the wells of salvation with joy and say with the psalmist, "we will triumph in Thy salvation, and in the name of our God we will set up our banners" (Psalm 20:5).

Being a Christian is not meant to be a miserable, long-faced, sanctimonious profession; it is a joyful life to be known and lived like Christ's. May we so live and act that others may see in us this joy so that they, like the Queen of Sheba, may truly be able to say: "Happy are thy men, happy are these thy servants, which stand continually before thee, and that hear thy wisdom" (1 Kings 10:8).

Haven't we known the happiness of them "whose transgression is forgiven, whose sin is covered" and also the happiness of "the man whom Thou choosest, and causest to approach unto Thee"? Haven't we been comforted in Zion, the place of God's choice and haven't we found it to be a place "like the garden of the LORD; joy and gladness shall be found therein, thanksgiving and the voice of melody" (Isaiah 51:3)? Therefore, "Rejoice in the Lord alway: again I will say, rejoice" (Philippians 4:4).

CHAPTER NINE: THE PRESENT MINISTRY AND WORK OF CHRIST IN HEAVEN

———

The present ministry of the Lord Jesus Christ in heaven is a theme of absorbing interest. His work in resurrection glory is vast and comprehensive in its scope. We may try to explore in measure the work of Christ in sustaining the vast universe and all the things in it. They were brought into existence by His word and are upheld and sustained; His almighty power is inherent in His word, and the vast universe is subject to His omnipotent will and word: "Upholding all things by the word of His power" (Hebrews 1:8). Everything, everywhere, is dependent for its present existence upon Him and the effectiveness of His word of power. It is a constant witness to the existence of Christ in resurrection glory and power that all things continue in ordered movement and place, undeviating in their course to fulfill the divine will. "And in Him all things consist" (Colossians 1:17).

It is a theme which should cause our hearts to be bowed in adoring wonder and humble worship, for what are we in this vast array of created things to be thought of at all? And yet, as the hymn writer puts it:

"All things living He doth feed,

His full hand supplies their need;

For His mercies aye endure,

Ever faithful, ever sure."

Not only does He sustain the universe, but He is mindful of the needs of all His creatures: "He watereth the mountains from His chambers: the earth is satisfied with the fruit of Thy works, He causeth the grass to grow for the cattle, and herb for the service of man; that He may bring forth food out of the earth: and wine that maketh glad the heart of man, and oil to make his face to shine, and bread that strengtheneth man's heart" (Psalm 104:13-15).

The millions of the human race are supplied with the necessities of life by the operation of those laws which men call the laws of nature, but which are in fact the laws of God functioning through Him who is the power and wisdom of God both in creation and redemption. Little do men think that they are dependent for their daily bread upon the One whom this world cast out and rejected. Likewise, the vast kingdom of the animal creation, the birds of the air and the fish of the sea, are all provided for by His beneficent hand (see Psalm 104). Apart from the exercise of the power of Christ upon the throne of heaven in thus supplying the needs of all living beings and creatures in this world, scientific ingenuity would utterly fail to make provision for them.

If we should think, additionally, of the spiritual needs of fallen humanity, then we find that "there is ... one Mediator also between God and men, Himself Man, Christ Jesus." He was between God and men on the Cross to effect reconciliation. His work is a completed work in that respect, but the application to the needs of men of that work is something which goes on

throughout time. "Him did God exalt with His right hand to
be a Prince and a Saviour" (Acts 5:81). He is now in the glory
of heaven - "Jesus the Mediator of a new covenant" (Hebrews
12:24), and "the Mediator of a better covenant, which has been
enacted upon better promises" (Hebrews 8:6). He has ratified
that better covenant by blood and now lives in the power of
an indissoluble life to administer its terms to those who comply
with it, whether it be the sinner coming for salvation, or the
believer responding to the terms of that covenant by practical
obedience. The work of the Lord Jesus goes on forever in this
respect.

THE BUILDING OF THE CHURCH

We remember His word in Matthew 16 where in anticipation
He says, "and upon this Rock I will build My Church; and the
gates of Hades shall not prevail against it." In 1 Corinthians
12:18 it says, "For in one Spirit were we all baptized into one
Body," which is described as "the Church, which is His Body"
in Ephesians 1:21-22. The work of building this Church goes on
throughout this dispensation and is the work of the Lord Jesus
in heaven; it is He who takes believing sinners and baptizes them
into One Body. He is its Nourisher, Cherisher, and Preserver.
He is the Head of the Church, controlling and fashioning that
wonderful structure according to God's eternal purpose. He is
also "Head over all things to the Church," supplying its every
necessity as He awaits the glorious moment of presentation to
Himself of that which will be eternally "the fullness of Him that
filleth all in all".

PREPARING A PLACE FOR YOU

Who has not pondered and reveled in the sweetness and preciousness of the promise: "I go to prepare a place for you. And if I go and prepare a place for you, I come again, and will receive you unto Myself; that where I am, there ye may be also" (John 14:2-3)? What comfort to our hearts in this squalid scene of earth with all its sorrow and trouble to know that amidst the many abiding places in that land of glory, there is "a place" being prepared by Him for us, "for you"! Can we not hear the beating of that heart of infinite love in those breathings of prayer? "Father, that which Thou hast given Me, I will that, where I am, they also may be with Me; that they may behold My glory, which Thou hast given Me" (John 17:24).

Yes, He who has bought us at infinite cost at Calvary is engaged in preparing "a place" for us. He is longing and waiting for that glorious day when He will see us all in that wondrous abode. Are we expectant and longing to the degree that we may be able to say in truth like John, "Amen! Come, Lord Jesus"?

"Blest words to those through pain and sorrow wading,

'Tis to My Father's house I needs must go,

There to prepare a place where joy unfading

In Mine own presence ye may ever know."

THE ADVOCATE

Meanwhile we are left for a little while on this earth to bear testimony for Him. Amongst the pitfalls and snares that dog our paths, how often we stumble and fall, how we fail and fall short in the way of life required of us because of the activities of our evil nature. Indeed we would be totally downcast and give up the struggle, but for the assurance that "we have an Advocate with the Father, Jesus Christ the Righteous." His present work as Advocate in heaven is on behalf of all God's failing children who come to God in confession. He is able to present before His Father, because of His shed blood and His inherent and manifested righteous character, an unfailing plea for the forgiveness of God's erring children, so that: "if we confess our sins, he is faithful and righteous to forgive us our sins, and to cleanse us from all unrighteousness" (1 John 1:9).

Because of the advocacy of our Lord Jesus Christ before the Father on our behalf, we may know the precious words "He restoreth my soul" and so we may go on in happy communion with God.

THE LORD'S SHEPHERD CARE

Whilst every individual sheep may share in the Shepherd's love and care, there are certainly blessings which they can never know apart from obedience to His will. He is the Good Shepherd who died for them, He is the Great Shepherd who lives for them. He is also the Chief Shepherd, the Shepherd of the Flock, but many of the sheep never know the joy of being gathered into His Flock; they have never responded to His call to separation to Him outside the camp. The Flock is a gathered, known and numbered people together on earth by His call. To be one of His sheep requires simple faith in Him as Saviour, but to be in the

Flock requires obedience to His will. Scattered sheep are not a flock; a flock is made up of gathered sheep under the care and guidance of the Shepherd.

The Lord called and gathered His own sheep from the fold of John, Then He says, "Other sheep I have which are not of this fold: them also I must bring and they shall hear My voice; and they shall become one flock". Scripture never speaks of flocks, but one flock with reference to His gathered people. The words of Peter in 1 Peter 5:2-3 are relevant; when writing to the elders in the five provinces he says "Tend the flock of God which is among you, making yourselves examples to the flock". They could never tend that flock unless it was known, gathered and accessible. They were to do this work of tending under the Chief Shepherd in heaven; it was His ministry to His gathered people through the under-shepherds, because there is only one Shepherd. It is His care, His guidance, His will that the under-shepherds are to express, not their own; they are but under-shepherds, men under authority, called, fitted and engaged in this work of expressing the desires of the perfect Shepherd who is now in heaven.

It is a work which springs from love toward the Chief Shepherd and His voice should always be heard in heart-searching power by them: "Lovest thou Me?" "Feed My lambs"; "Tend My sheep"; "Feed My sheep." And so we see a ministry of shepherd care directed from the resurrected Lord toward the flock of God through overseers or elders, and these are responsible to the Chief Shepherd for their work and actions; they are to be subject to Him who has entrusted them with this great work, and also to subject themselves, the younger to the elder, as instructed in

1 Peter 5:5, as examples to the flock. They are to minister to the spiritual needs of God's people, to care for them, to guide, counsel, reprove, rebuke, exhort with all longsuffering, remembering that the sheep are those for whom Christ died; they are His sheep. They are to feed with food convenient to the lambs and sheep of the flock by healthful Spirit-given ministry.

With tender hand and loving heart, they are to help the weak and feeble and encourage the fainthearted, and such work must be done with a single eye to God's glory and the blessing of His people. They are to be men of courage who will stand against the attacks of the Adversary, steadfast in their faith, prepared to spend and be spent, to defend the sheep, and stand in defence of the gospel and of the faith once for all delivered to the saints; men who put God's people and God's honour first, and themselves last, men who can pray in truth as Solomon did: "Give Thy servant therefore an understanding heart to judge Thy people, that I may discern between good and evil; for who is able to judge this Thy great people?" (1 Kings 3:9). Besides the Shepherd care and ministry of the Lord through overseers to the flock, there is His present work as Son over God's house and also His work as Great Priest over the house of God.

CHRIST AS SON OVER GOD'S HOUSE

This subject is worthy of close attention as it relates to the ecclesiastical position of all believers. Before we can appreciate the position which Christ has as Son over God's house, we must first define what the house of God is. It is a sad fact that, of the vast numbers of believers in the world today, comparatively few have any conception of this precious truth. Those who may have are often so bound up with tradition, friendships or family relationships that they are unable to give expression to it. We freely admit that for a disciple of the Lord Jesus to take his or her place in the house of God may demand a sacrifice which perhaps few are prepared to make. The majority takes the easy way and the popular path regardless of the word, "Buy the truth, and sell it not" (Proverbs 23:28).

The house of God today is a spiritual house. During the life of the Lord Jesus on earth there was a material temple, and it is evident that the two could not exist as God's dwelling place at the same time. Indeed, the prophecy of Caiaphas makes it clear that: "Jesus should die for the nation; and not for the nation only, but that He might also gather together into one the children of God which are scattered abroad" (John 11:52).

There was to be the commencement of a new thing after the death of Christ and the Lord had this in view when He prayed that memorable prayer of John 17: "Neither for these only do I pray, but for them also that believe on Me through their word; that they may all be one ... that the world may believe ... that the world may know that Thou didst send Me."

It is quite clear from this that the Lord had before Him a visible oneness which was to be a witness of divine truth before the world and so He prayed, "Sanctify them in the truth: Thy word is truth." Concerning the material temple in Jerusalem He ultimately declared "Behold, your house is left unto you desolate" (Matthew 23:38).

A dispensation was about to commence after the death of Christ, which in contrast to the material things of the law, was to be spiritual in its character and manifestation. The cross was to be the means first of all of bringing men into eternal union with God, a union which can never be broken, for every believer stands perfect and complete in Christ. This is a union of life, of all who are sharers of a common salvation. This invisible union in Christ has been made the basis of church fellowship by many, though this has not the slightest foundation in Scripture. Believers are not gathered in testimony on the basis of their sanctification in Christ Jesus, but because of their sanctification in the truth, and this requires obedience to the truth.

The first example in scripture of a divinely called church which was "of God" clearly shows that its constitution was based upon acceptance and practice of, and adherence to, the truth: "They then that received his word were baptized ... and ... were added. And they continued steadfastly in the apostle's teaching and fellowship, in the breaking of bread and the prayers" (Acts 2:41-42).

Likewise, "the Corinthians hearing, believed and were baptized" (Acts 18:8). They were called out (2 Corinthians 6:17) and they were also called in - "into the Fellowship of His Son, Jesus Christ our Lord" (1 Corinthians 1:9). So, they became "the church of God in Corinth", "God's building" and the "temple of God" (see 1 Corinthians 3:16-17 and 2 Corinthians 6:16). Consequently, the obligations of collective responsibility rested upon them to cleanse the house or temple of which they formed a part according to the word: "Put away the wicked man from among yourselves" (1 Corinthians 5:18). In God's house there is a correct standard of behaviour, even as Paul wrote to Timothy: "That thou mayest know how men ought to behave themselves in the house of God, which is the church of the living God, the pillar and ground of the truth" (1 Timothy 3:15).

So the pillar of witness is set up among those who are sanctified in the truth and who hold and practice the truth relative to collective testimony and worship. From what we have said, it should be quite clear that the house of God is not something based on life in Christ alone; knowledge of, adherence to, and practice of the truth as seen in the above scriptures are also necessary.

Having shown that the house of God is a conditional unity of obedient disciples of the Lord, we proceed to show that Christ is Son in authority over the house of God. In this "He hath been counted worthy of more glory than Moses". Moses was indeed faithful in all God's house as a servant. He received divine instruction and never deviated from that word nor substituted his own will: "Thus did Moses: according to all that the LORD commanded him, so did he." But Christ is the Originator and Builder of the house, being faithful to Him that appointed Him, though He uses men in this work of building (see Psalm 127:1 and Acts 7:47. The material He procured by means of His cross-work He fashioned by His teaching of "the things concerning the kingdom of God" in resurrection. He commanded His disciples to preach, baptize and teach everything that He had commanded them; and to enable them to do so, He promised they would be clothed with power from on high. On the day of Pentecost Peter declared, "he hath poured forth this, which ye see and hear," and so the work of the risen Lord went on in the preparation of a habitation for God.

The theme of Peter's preaching that day was the resurrection, ascension and exaltation of Christ, whom God hath made both Lord and Christ. Three thousand souls that day bowed to His claims and Lordship and were added to that divinely recognised community found together in obedience to His word. They set apart Christ as Lord in their hearts, recognizing that God had given to Him all authority in heaven and on earth. The Lord in heaven used human instruments to accomplish His purposes and disciples obeyed their absent and now glorified Lord. They worked and walked by faith in the consciousness of His promise, "Lo, I am with you always, even unto the end of the world" (Matthew 28:20). The house was built; His people were gathered for whom He had died, "Who gave Himself for us, that He might redeem us from all iniquity, and purify unto Himself a people for His own, possession, zealous of good works" (Titus 2:14).

Thus living stones were builded together into a spiritual house by coming to Him, the Stone rejected by men, but precious to God. That Stone is now laid in the heavenly Zion, with all authority. He rules as Son over God's house; as Son He has been placed over all. Being the Founder, Architect, and Builder of the house, He has more glory than the house. Wouldn't it be wonderful if believers today would recognize the place that God has given Him and take their place under Him in God's house which is composed of churches of God fitly framed together into a holy temple in the Lord" (see 1 Corinthians 3:9 and Ephesians 2:21)?

In the first three chapters of the book of Revelation, we see the Lord walking in the midst of the seven golden lampstands, which are seven churches. As Son over God's house He is seen judging, rebuking, encouraging, warning and promising. He sees and knows, not as an outward observer, but as One who possesses a perfect knowledge of the motives and intents of the heart. He is concerned with their inward spiritual condition as well as with the place they occupy as golden lampstands. Position and condition should go together, and with Him they cannot be divorced. May we ponder over His heart-searching words to those churches so that we, too, may have a heart of wisdom and be found among those who tremble at His word. He is our one and only Lord. He is absent and unseen by mortal eye now, but He has said, "Behold I come quickly: hold fast that which thou hast Hold fast till I come" (Revelation 3:11; 2:25).

CHAPTER TEN: THE GREAT PRIEST OVER THE HOUSE OF GOD

─────

There is generally much confusion of thought about the Lord's ministry as priest, yet words could not be clearer than those found in Hebrews 10:21-22, "Having a Great Priest over the house of God; let us draw near." There are some who think that each company or assembly of believers which comes together to break bread is a house of God, in which case there would be numerous houses of God throughout the world. Scripture does not say that the Lord is Priest over the houses of God, but over the house (singular). Scripture teaches that there is only one house of God, composed of all churches of God. Where in the New Testament is any mention made of houses of God relative to God's together people? There are many churches of God, but only one house of God, and this should speak volumes to seekers after truth.

In Peter's first epistle to those in the five provinces of Pontus, Galatia, Cappadocia, Asia and Bithynia, are described as being "built up a spiritual house, to be a holy priesthood, to offer up spiritual sacrifices, acceptable to God through Jesus Christ" (1 Peter 1:1 and 2:5). No one could reasonably suppose that in such a large area there were not many churches of God, and these are in view in the exhortation to overseers, "Neither as lording it over the charge allotted to you" (1 Peter 5:8), yet the whole together is spoken of as one thing, "a spiritual house", "a holy priesthood" and "a holy nation". Peter indicates this when he says, "Ye also ... are built up a spiritual house."

John, in writing to the seven churches in Asia says "and he made us to be a kingdom, to be priests unto His God and Father" (Revelation 1:6). These seven churches were therefore in one kingdom and John himself, who was in the Isle of Patmos, was a partaker with them in that kingdom (verse 9). In these scriptures, we see the truth of one house, one kingdom and one priesthood. The same persons constitute the house, kingdom, and priesthood. In the typology of the past the same principles are seen: "Now therefore, if ye will obey My voice indeed, and keep My covenant, then ye shalt be a peculiar treasure unto Me from among all peoples: for all the earth is Mine: and ye shall be unto Me a kingdom of priests, and an holy nation" (Exodus 19:5-6).

When Israel had solemnly undertaken to obey God's voice, saying "All that the LORD hath spoken we will do, and be obedient," then, upon these conditions, God took them into covenant relationship, recognized them as His people and as a kingdom of priests, and made provision for them to fulfil their obligations and functions in association with the LORD'S dwelling place, for He said: "Let them make Me a sanctuary; that I may dwell among them" (Exodus 25:8), and again: "See ... that thou make all things according to the pattern that was shewed thee in the mount" (Hebrews 8:5).

God would not dwell in a tabernacle of human design, nor be served by men in a system of human origin. His will and way must be paramount. Let us learn the lesson. The conditional character of the house, kingdom and priesthood was thus set forth, and so it is today, "Whose house are we, if we hold fast." Christ is both Son and Priest over the house of God. As Son He imparts a glory and dignity to the house worthy of the One whose house it is. He is the supreme example and living exponent of godliness (1 Timothy 3:16), hence the demands upon those in God's house to "follow after godliness." The standard of God's house is high and human frailty is ever present; hence the need for a Priest over God's house.

There are two spheres of service associated with God's house: (1) to man in testimony, in connection with which prayer is vital, and (2) to God, in holy priesthood service in praise. In both spheres, the Lord Jesus renders service as priest over God's house. In the epistle to the Hebrews He is seen bringing many sons to glory through a hostile world; He is their princely Leader, and at the same time the High Priest of their confession. In the past, Israel's confession was bound up with the law given by Moses - which they undertook to keep. Today it is bound up with "the faith once for all delivered to the saints" which they are responsible to hold and contend for.

It would have been utterly impossible for Israel to maintain their status as a peculiar people and a kingdom of priests apart from the work of the high priest of their confession, even Aaron. He stood between the people and God in his work of making atonement for the holy place, the tent of meeting, the altar and for all the assembly of Israel, by which the relationship of a weak and failing people was maintained with God. So also our High Priest by the all-sufficiency of His sacrifice and acceptability as Priest is able to make propitiation for the sins of the people, i.e., God's together-people (see Hebrews 2:17). He maintains the sanctity and righteousness of God's holy throne in faithfulness and is able also to meet the needs of a failing people in mercy. With true sympathy, He can enter into the difficulties and temptations besetting the path of the sanctified and faithful, and "He is able to succour them that are tempted."

Indeed, "He is able to save to the uttermost them that draw near to God through Him," otherwise, the wilderness of this world would be strewn with the spiritual wreckage of countless lives of God's saints. We cannot go on without Him; He is our Hope in God's presence; all our resources are in Him who is after the order of Melchizedek, of whom it is written that he was "priest of God Most High possessor of heaven and earth," and He has gone into God's presence on our behalf. This hope we have as an anchor of the soul. If we fail to lay hold of this Hope we shall drift and fall away from the living God. May we know increasingly by experience the value of this wondrous ministry of our High Priest!

"Having then a Great High Priest, who hath passed through the heavens, Jesus the Son of God, let us hold fast our confession. Let us therefore draw near with boldness unto the throne of grace, that we may receive mercy, and may find grace to help us in time of need" (Hebrews 4:14-16).

The Lord Jesus is also Priest over God's house as they draw near as worshippers. In His incarnation He sought worshippers for His Father; in His resurrection as a Priest He is over the kingdom of priests. Aaron was over the kingdom of priests in the past, being divinely called and authorized to act on behalf of the nation in their approach to God. No sacrifice could ever reach the divine presence apart from the ministry of the high priest, so also it is impossible for those in God's house to bring their offerings to God with acceptance apart from Him who is Priest over God's house.

In the law, clear and precise instructions are given relative to the sacrifices which were to be brought, the place to which they were to be brought, and the manner of their presentation. In these matters Aaron the priest was to "teach the children of Israel all the statutes which the LORD hath spoken unto them by the hand of Moses," so that they should put a difference between the holy and the common, and between the unclean and the clean (Leviticus 10:10-11). "For the priest's lips should keep knowledge, and they should seek the law at his mouth: for he is the messenger of the LORD of Hosts" (Malachi 2:7).

The Great Priest over God's house is the Divine Instructor through the Holy Spirit. This may be implied in the words of Acts 1:1, "The former treatise I made, O Theophilus, concerning all that Jesus began to do and to teach", so that in resurrection He continues to do and also to teach, though He does so by the work of the Holy Spirit through men. At this point it may be well to note the difference between the house of God and the holy place, or Holies. The house of God is composed of the Lord's obedient disciples in churches of God, such as the church of God in Corinth which could be "known and read of all men" and the church in Antioch which could be called together when so desired (see 2 Corinthians 3:2; Acts 14:27), or "may come together in the church" (1 Corinthians 11:18); all this shows saints together on earth.

It was this people who were addressed collectively in Hebrews 10:19, as "having ... boldness to enter into the holy place by the blood of Jesus." The holy place therefore is not the house of God, nor is it the meeting room or hall where the church gathers. The holy place or holies is where a holy priesthood may enter "to offer up spiritual sacrifices." It is in heaven, where the High Priest is seen as "a minister of the sanctuary." It is there that we are exhorted to "draw near ... having a Great Priest over the house of God", and right of access by the blood of Jesus, to worship in spirit and in -truth, and to fill the hands of our High Priest - for it is necessary that this High Priest also should have somewhat to offer. The way into the Holies has been secured by the death, resurrection and ascension of the Lord Jesus into heaven, but in our entering in we must be in that right spiritual condition essential for such service, for: "Who shall ascend into the hill of the LORD? And who shall stand in His holy place? He that hath clean hands and a pure heart" (Psalm 24:3-4).

Let us cleanse ourselves then from all defilement of flesh and spirit and, "Through Him ... let us offer up a sacrifice of praise to God continually, that is, the fruit of lips which make confession to His Name" (Hebrews 13:15). We know that whatever we may offer is imperfect by reason of our imperfect thought and apprehension, but we are assured that through Him who bears the iniquity of our holy things, and who is Himself the Leader of the praise in the great congregation, our praises are "acceptable to God through Jesus Christ."

Did you love *The Glories and the Excellencies of Christ*? Then you should read *Blood Most Precious - A Bible Study*[1] by EDWIN NEELY!

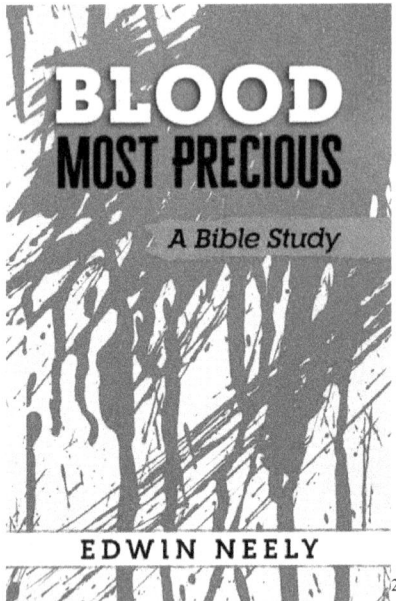

With no less than 375 Bible verses on the subject of blood, God definitely has something important to tell us about it. In this informative book, Edwin Neely explains its role and meaning under both the Old and New Covenants and its significance to us as Christians today – not just in our salvation, but in our service as well.

CHAPTER ONE: NON-SACRIFICIAL BLOOD

1. https://books2read.com/u/bzpMrZ

2. https://books2read.com/u/bzpMrZ

Also by F. McCormick

The Glories and the Excellencies of Christ

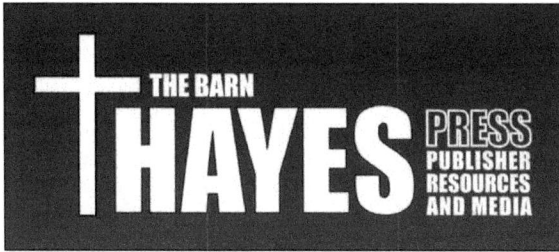

About the Publisher

Hayes Press (www.hayespress.org) is a registered charity in the United Kingdom, whose primary mission is to disseminate the Word of God, mainly through literature. It is one of the largest distributors of gospel tracts and leaflets in the United Kingdom, with over 100 titles and hundreds of thousands despatched annually. In addition to paperbacks and eBooks, Hayes Press also publishes Plus Eagles Wings, a fun and educational Bible magazine for children, and Golden Bells, a popular daily Bible reading calendar in wall or desk formats. Also available are over 100 Bibles in many different versions, shapes and sizes, Bible text posters and much more!

www.ingramcontent.com/pod-product-compliance
Lightning Source LLC
Chambersburg PA
CBHW071925020426
42331CB00010B/2733